A DAY IN AN
ECOSYSTEM

24
HOURS
IN AN
ESTUARY

LAURA L. SULLIVAN

Published in 2018 by Cavendish Square Publishing, LLC
243 5th Avenue, Suite 136, New York, NY 10016

Copyright © 2018 by Cavendish Square Publishing, LLC

First Edition

CPSIA Compliance Information: Batch #CS17CSQ

All websites were available and accurate when this book was sent to press.

Library of Congress Cataloging-in-Publication Data

Names: Sullivan, Laura L..

Title: 24 hours in an estuary / Laura L. Sullivan.

Description: New York : Cavendish Square, 2018. | Series: A day in an ecosystem | Includes index.

Identifiers: ISBN 9781502624864 (library bound) | ISBN 9781502624871 (ebook)

Subjects: LCSH: Estuarine ecology--Juvenile literature. | Estuarine biology--Juvenile literature. | Estuaries--Juvenile literature.

Classification: LCC QH541.5.E8 C34 2018 | DDC 577.7'86--dc23

Editorial Director: David McNamara
Editor: Fletcher Doyle
Copy Editor: Rebecca Rohan
Associate Art Director: Amy Greenan
Designer: Stephanie Flecha
Production Coordinator: Karol Szymczuk
Photo Research: J8 Media

Printed in the United States of America

CONTENTS

DAWN

ALL through the night you have been paddling your kayak down the Hillsborough River in Tampa, Florida. Guided by the full moon and starlight, you've gone past a huge city and also through a wilderness of cypress and palm trees. When you shine your flashlight across the surface of the river, you see the glinting eyes of alligators reflected in the beam. The freshwater is tea-colored and full of **nutrients** from **decaying** vegetation. The current flows swiftly. As the first light of dawn touches the eastern sky behind you, everything changes. You are paddling into Tampa Bay, Florida's biggest open-water **estuary** environment.

The sharp smell of salt water hits your nose, and you realize you've entered a zone where freshwater and salt water meet. This is the place where the Hillsborough River flows into the Gulf of Mexico. It is a region of change, where the temperature, **salinity** (amount of salt in the water), and visibility shift from hour to hour. And yet, it is home to more than two

As you paddle from the river to saltwater, you will learn about life in an estuary.

An estuary is a place where a river meets the sea.

hundred species of fish and many other species that make Tampa Bay, and other estuaries, among the most valuable **marine ecosystems** on the planet.

As you paddle slowly into the estuary, you see that it has aspects of both the river and the salt water bay. Nutrients come from both directions. Rich decaying matter is washed into the estuary from the river, and fish, **invertebrates**, **larva**, and **plankton** bring nutrients from the Gulf of Mexico. Freshwater mixes with salt water, creating a zone of **brackish** water. The salinity changes from place to place in the estuary. The constant exchange of water brings **sediment**, too, which can hold nutrients, but can also cloud the water.

You see so much life around you. Mullet leap in the shifting **tide**, while Atlantic bottlenose dolphins chase them. Pelicans soar overhead in a V-formation, while an osprey dives for a speckled sea trout near the **mangroves**. Endangered wading birds such as reddish

Beluga whales inhabit the Gulf of Ob, a cold water estuary.

THE GULF OF OB

The Gulf of Ob, where Russia's Ob River flows into the Arctic Ocean, is an example of one of the coldest estuaries. It is also the longest estuary, stretching about 600 miles (1,000 kilometers). Beluga whales travel to that **frigid** estuary every year to hunt for fish.

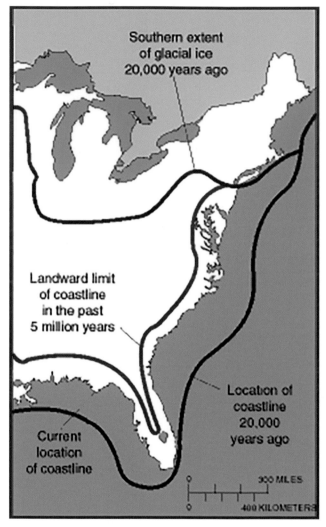

Changing water levels over thousands of years helped to form estuaries.

egrets **forage** for crustaceans on the sand flats. Blue crabs move sideways through thickets of seagrass, past blue-eyed scallops and **camouflaged** sea horses. A woman wearing high rubber waders pries oysters from their bed, tossing them into a bucket. Life abounds here. Yet, the conditions that make such abundant life possible also present challenges. Not every kind of marine life can thrive in the estuaries.

Most estuaries around the world are about ten thousand years old. Before that, sea levels were low because some of Earth's oceans were stored in **glaciers** during the last **ice age**. Then the ice melted and sea levels began to rise. River valleys became flooded by the rising sea, and estuaries were created. (Other estuaries were created by glacier movement, or by the shifting of Earth's **tectonic plates**.)

As you explore the Tampa Bay estuary at the break of dawn, you think about how it's like other estuaries around the world. There is a large estuary at the mouth of the Amazon, the world's largest river. Farther north, Chesapeake Bay in Maryland and Virginia is the largest estuary in the United States. In England, there is a cold-water estuary where the Thames River meets the North Sea. Although the environments differ, each estuary shares the characteristic of being a unique ecosystem where freshwater and salt water meet.

MORNING

AS you paddle through Tampa Bay in the growing light of sunrise, you see what first looks like a **reef**. Moving closer, you see that it is actually a cluster of oysters. They have grown in a mound that looks almost like a coral reef, with baby oysters growing on the shells of generations of old oysters. At low tide, some of the oysters stick out of the water. The layers of oysters have formed an ecosystem. Oyster reefs provide homes for many other animals, such as barnacles, mussels, worms, and small fish. Crabs, rays, and some seabirds eat oysters. Oysters are found in many estuaries.

This morning, you see a strange cloud in the water all around the reef. Summertime and hot water signals the start of the oysters' reproductive season. Females release clouds of up to one hundred million eggs each year, while males launch **sperm** into the water. If they meet, and the eggs are **fertilized**, the eggs will develop into larva. These tiny baby oysters

Oysters are a favorite food of many estuary animals—and also humans.

MAKING A HOME

Seagrasses can create their own perfect environment. They trap sediments floating in the water. Those sediments fall down to their roots, making the ground level rise. This brings the seagrass bed closer to the surface and the sun. Every generation is a little shallower and can get more solar energy.

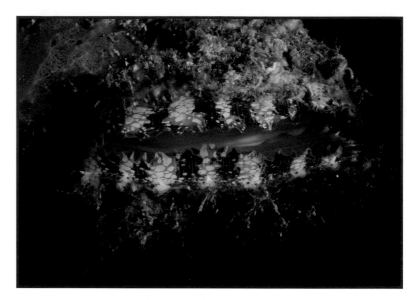

Oysters clean water by filtering it through their gills.

float until they land on the right surface. They are attracted to areas that have other oysters. They often won't latch on until they detect that they are in or near an existing oyster bed. When they attach, the babies are called **spats**.

You see oysters of all sizes on the reef. Some of them are undergoing a **transformation** as they grow. In the first year of their lives, when they are smaller, they are males, because making sperm requires less energy. When they grow bigger, they transform into females. Now they have the size and energy to make millions of eggs.

Oysters are filter feeders. You can see that many have their shells open now. They eat by taking water in through their **gills** and filtering plankton and small particles out. The nutrients are digested, and other particles are expelled as waste. Once the particles—which may include pollutants and fertilizer—are expelled, they sit inactive in the sediment and no longer cloud the water.

Oysters help keep estuaries clean. Each oyster can filter up to 50 gallons (189 liters) of water a day. Tampa Bay looks clean after a long effort to restore the region. Other estuaries still need work. Once, there were so many oysters in Chesapeake Bay that they could filter all the water in the estuary every day. Now, there are fewer oysters. It takes about a year for the remaining oysters to do the same task.

As the sun rises fully, you look around Tampa Bay and realize that it is huge—about 400 square

Many creatures, such as this green sea turtle, can be found in seagrass beds.

Scallop numbers have declined because of shark overfishing.

EVERYTHING IS CONNECTED

Bay scallops are commonly found in estuary seagrass beds. Their numbers have been getting smaller for an unusual reason: overfishing of sharks. Stingrays are one of the main **predators** of scallops. Many sharks, such as hammerheads, feed on rays. With fewer sharks, stingray populations have increased, and they are eating more scallops. A ban on or reduction of shark fishing could restore the balance.

miles (1,036 sq km). Yet, when you plunge your paddle straight down, it hits the bottom. In most parts of the estuary, if the sun is bright and the water is clear, you can see to the bottom. The average water depth is only 12 feet (3.7 m). Many of the plants and animals that live here need to be in shallow water, because they depend on the sun.

You leave the oyster reef and head toward a place where the clear water grows darker. As you get close to it, you see something waving underwater. It looks almost like tall grass swaying in the wind. These marine plants are not seaweeds, which are algae. They are actual flowering plants called seagrass. Some common types include turtle grass, manatee grass, and shoal grass. These plants have to live in shallow water, because they rely on the sun for **photosynthesis**.

You see many species of animals in the seagrass bed. Sea horses curl around seagrass stems. Their close relatives, the long skinny pipefish, align themselves with grass blades and move with the current so they look like seagrass themselves. Tiny pufferfish and filefish move about the grassy forest. Algae and small invertebrates grow on the leaves. In the sand below, you can see little crabs and shrimp eating dead vegetation.

Suddenly, you catch sight of a huge dark shape in the water near you. You are frightened because you know sharks, including the **aggressive**

A seahorse hides in blades of seagrass.

bull shark, sometimes feed in estuaries. But as the massive shape comes closer you hear a puff of breath and see a whiskery mouth break the surface. It is a manatee.

Manatees are large marine mammals that can reach about 12 feet (3.7 m) and 1,300 pounds (590 kilograms). Though they are also called sea cows, their closest relatives are elephants. As you watch the manatee start to eat the seagrass, you can understand the relationship. The manatee's lips are split. The left and right sides can move in different directions. They can grab the seagrass in much the same way an elephant would use the tip of its trunk to pluck leaves.

Manatees are one of many kinds of estuary animals that can move freely between freshwater and salt water. During the summer, manatees spend a lot of time in salt water, cruising in estuaries and even in the Gulf of Mexico and the Atlantic Ocean. In the winter, though, they leave the salt water and move into the spring-fed freshwater. Despite their

Manatees, which can live in both salt and freshwater, eat different kinds of seagrass.

This manatee and her nursing calf are at risk of cold shock if the water gets too chilly.

bulk, manatees don't have a layer of **blubber** like whales and dolphins do. If the water temperature dips below 68 degrees Fahrenheit (20 degrees Celsius), manatees can die, because their digestive systems shut down in the cold. Near the freshwater springs, though, the water stays a constant 72°F (22°C).

AFTERNOON

IT is past noon on a sweltering summer day, and you wipe the sweat from your forehead as you explore the Tampa Bay estuary. If you are hot, so are some of the animals living underwater. The shallow water of the estuary warms every day in the sun. Some animals thrive in the warmer water. Active, strong fish that get **sluggish** at night when it is colder become more active as the water and their muscles get warmer. Most fish are cold-blooded and rely on their environment to regulate their body temperature. Fish may bask in clear, shallow, sunny places to warm. Others may seek the deep shade of mangrove roots to cool down on a hot afternoon. Some fish and invertebrates even burrow under the sand, where the temperature remains more constant.

You can hear splashes all around you. At first, you can't tell what is jumping, but before long you catch sight of a solid, silvery fish between one and two feet long. It is a mullet, which are active in the heat of the

Creatures such as these garden eels can retreat under the sand for safety or to cool down.

Left: The vegetarian mullet is a common fish that many other animals eat.
Right: Mullet often jump, though scientists aren't completely sure why.

afternoon. Scientists aren't sure why mullet jump. Sometimes they do it to avoid predators, but other times they jump when nothing is hunting them. It might be to shake loose parasites, to gulp air to increase their oxygen intake, or even as a form of communication.

Seeing the mullet makes you curious. When you were on the river, you also saw lots of mullet. How can they move from freshwater to salt water? Most of the time, if you put a freshwater fish in salt water, it will die. If you put a saltwater fish in freshwater, it also will die. Yet in your kayak journey, you saw many of the same kinds of fish in both the freshwater river, and in the brackish, salt water estuary. Not only the mullet, but also snook, flounder, jacks, and several species of sharks and rays routinely move between the estuary and the river.

Saltwater and freshwater fish have different ways of dealing with **osmosis**, or the way that liquid moves through a membrane, such as the fish's gills. Water moves from an area with less salt to an area with more salt, trying to balance both sides. All living things have some salt in their blood and tissues. A freshwater fish's body is saltier inside than the water around it, so freshwater is always moving into its body. A freshwater fish absorbs too much water and has to get rid of it through urine.

Flounder can survive in both freshwater and salt water, and often move into rivers and springs.

MANGROVE SEEDS

Most plants make a seed that falls off the plant and then stays dormant (not developing) until it is ready to **germinate**. However, mangrove seeds germinate while still attached to the parent plant. They have "live young" like animals do. They grow an attached, mature plant that is capable of photosynthesis and then drop it into the water. It will float for weeks or months until it finds a good place to root.

Osmosis is the way in which water moves through a membrane, such as a fish's gills.

A saltwater fish, on the other hand, is less salty inside its body than its environment. It is always in danger of losing water from its body to the saltwater outside. A saltwater fish has to drink a lot of water to compensate. It can also expel some salt through its gills.

Most fish have to live in either salt water or freshwater. Here in the estuary there are many fish that can choose either one. These are called **euryhaline** fish. They can move from salt water to freshwater and back again. They can also survive in brackish estuaries. Being able to move from the river to the estuary has advantages. Most predators can't follow the fish into the river, and there are often fewer freshwater predators. Euryhaline fish can also move back and forth to take advantage of more food sources.

As you watch a silvery school of mullet feeding, you suddenly see a snook dart out and grab one, swallowing it in one gulp. You recognize the snook by its protruding lower jaw, and the single dark stripe running from

Osmosis

neck to tail. Snook are a species that depends on estuaries for survival. Adult snook can live in any salinity, but young snook have to travel to fresh or brackish river and estuary waters while they grow up. After the snook gobbles the mullet, it retreats to the cool shade of the thick forest of mangroves that lines much of Tampa Bay.

Mangroves are one of the few species of trees that can live in salty conditions. Some kinds live with their roots mostly under the salt

Snook are one of the fish that can move back and forth from freshwater to salt water.

DOLPHINS

Bottlenose dolphins, the most common kind of dolphin, are often found in estuaries. They can use the shallow water of estuaries to hunt for food. Dolphins work in teams to chase fish into shallow water. There, the fish can't escape easily. Dolphins can partly leave the water, rolling on their sides in shallow seagrass beds or mud flats to get the stranded fish.

Red mangroves have arching roots that let them survive even at high tide.

water. These tropical plants are common up and down the Florida coastline, as far north as the freeze zone. Red mangroves have high, arching roots. It looks almost like the tree is standing on spider legs.

This mangrove community is vital to the estuary. The arching roots provide a perfect place for baby fish to hide. Big predators can't get through the tangle of roots. Many fish depend on estuary mangrove forests for their reproductive cycle. About 90 percent of commercially harvested fish in Florida rely on mangroves.

Mangroves are also home to many other species. You see tree-climbing mangrove crabs scuttling along the roots and blue crabs underwater. Mollusks such as lightning whelks travel slowly in the sand between the roots, leaving long trails behind them. When you look up, you see that several kinds of seabirds have made nests in the mangrove boughs. Pelicans, roseate spoonbills, and egrets all use the mangrove canopy for

Many birds, such as these brown pelicans, nest in mangroves.

their rookeries. This is a place where many build nests. You even see oysters growing on the roots, exposed at low tide. You've heard locals tell tourists that around here oysters grow on trees. Now you know what they mean!

EVENING

AS the sun sinks lower, you see more and more predators start to hunt. Most fish will feed at any time of the day. In an estuary, though, the shallow water can sometimes heat up a lot on a summer afternoon. Some fish wait for the rising sun to warm their bodies, but in the middle of the day, they can get too hot. Also, prey species can see predators in the direct sunlight. But by evening, the water has begun to cool, and the slanting sunlight creates confusing shadows that help predators hide. As the sky and water start to grow darker, predators are more likely to catch prey unaware.

Many types of sharks swim in estuaries. In Tampa Bay, for example, about a dozen species of sharks either live in or visit the estuary. Some come in search of food, following schools of mullet and other bait fish. Others use estuaries as their nurseries.

The bonnethead is a small type of hammerhead that is common in estuaries.

You see several dorsal fins cutting through the water and paddle over to check them out. It is a school of bonnethead sharks. These small members of the hammerhead family are common in warm waters of North and South America. They like seagrass beds and muddy or sandy areas, where they hunt for crustaceans. All sharks have sensors that can pick up electrical signals from other animals. Sharks in the hammerhead

Some sharks, rays, and skates lay egg cases, such as this "mermaid's purse" from a skate.

family have a head shape that probably makes them better at this. You watch the bonnetheads sweep their heads back and forth. They are scanning the sand underneath the seagrass. Suddenly one thrusts its head into the sand. You briefly see the flailing claw of an unlucky blue crab before it is gobbled down.

Bonnethead sharks are viviparous, which means their babies—or pups—are born alive. Most sharks and rays have live pups. Some, however, lay egg cases. You see something attached to a clump of seagrass—a black, leathery case a few inches long. It looks like it has horns on either end. It is the egg case of a skate, an animal that resembles a ray. The egg cases are sometimes called mermaid's purses. You've found it at just the right time. The egg case begins to move, and you see it split at one end. A baby skate wiggles out, its wing-like sides folded over. At once, it unfolds and swims off deeper into the seagrass, burrowing under the sand before it becomes a meal to a larger predator.

Larger sharks, such as the great hammerhead, which reaches a maximum of 20 feet (6 m) and more than 1,000 pounds (453 kg), also enter estuaries. However, they are seen more often in deeper places, such as the estuary mouth, or in channels. You spy a large shark fin in one of the deep, man-made channels that let large boats move safely through the estuary. It is a bull shark, a large, sometimes aggressive species. Bull sharks have been responsible for many shark bites.

Bull sharks are stocky, aggressive sharks that can survive hundreds of miles upriver in freshwater.

RIVER SHARKS

Bull sharks are one of the few shark species that can live in freshwater. They have been found hundreds of miles up rivers. They have been spotted up the Mississippi River as far as Illinois.

Fish aren't the only predators you see hunting in the waters of the Tampa Bay estuary as the sun starts to set. Humans share this environment with animals, and you see plenty of them searching for their own seafood. Some fish for recreation, such as the woman you see in another kayak. She is skimming close to the mangrove roots so she can cast her line for redfish. Others are commercial fishermen, who work the estuary waters to make a living. You see a pair of fishermen on a boat dropping crab traps overboard near oyster reefs and jetties.

Large sharks, such as the great hammerhead, sometimes visit estuaries.

Stone crabs are a very expensive food that is caught in estuaries.

A floating buoy marks the location of each one, so the crabber can check his or her traps in the morning. They are hoping to catch stone crabs. These may be caught only at certain times of the year, but they sell for a lot of money. Fishermen will snap off one or both claws and return the live animal to the estuary. Though some crabs don't survive, many do and will regrow their claws.

The world relies on estuaries for seafood. In the United States, most fish and shellfish used for food need estuaries to survive. Some, such as oysters, bay scallops, and blue crabs, live there full time. Many others, such as salmon, menhaden, and herring, need estuaries as part of their spawning, or as nurseries for juvenile fish. All told, about 75 percent of the fish caught in the United States for sale depends in part on estuaries. Estimates vary, but estuaries contribute more than $100 billion in economic benefit to the US economy. The money comes from fishing and tourism.

KELP FORESTS

An estuary environment unique to colder waters is the kelp forest. Kelp is a saltwater algae that can reach 200 feet (61 m) in height. It grows in a way that resembles giant seagrass and serves as a hiding place for many animals. Sea otters, seals, sea lions, and whales depend on some of the species found in kelp forests. It is common off California, such as in the San Francisco Bay estuary.

Many of the world's biggest cities, including New York City, are located on estuaries.

Humans have always lived near estuaries for their food and for their value in shipping and trade. Twenty-two of the thirty-two biggest cities in the world are located on estuaries. This means these ecosystems are always in danger from humans. Overfishing has reduced many fish and shellfish populations. Fertilizer runoff creates algae blooms that can kill marine life. Oil spills, plastic waste, and other pollution are constant threats. Bridges can restrict water

Volunteers, such as these people planting mangroves, work to preserve estuaries.

movement, disrupting the natural exchange of salt water and freshwater.

As evening turns to night, you think about what local groups are doing to protect estuaries. Tampa Bay, for example, lost about 80 percent of its seagrass beds over the last century. Seagrasses are an indicator of water quality and cleanness, because they can't survive well in polluted water. Dredging, construction near shore, and damage from boats also destroys seagrass. However, new policies are helping to keep the water clean and protect the estuary ecosystem. Volunteers have planted acres of new seagrasses. The Tampa Bay estuary is being preserved, but there is still a lot of work to do to protect the environment here, and in estuaries around the world.

NIGHT

THE sun has set, and the last light has gone. After a while, the moon rises in the east, huge and low in the sky. It casts a silvery glow over the estuary waters. During the day, you observed shorebirds feeding in various environments. They used different ways to locate small crabs, shrimp, sand fleas, marine worms, and mollusks. Some, like the reddish egret, chased after baitfish in shallow water, sprinting with outstretched wings. The great blue heron stood motionless in the mangroves, suddenly darting out its spearlike beak to catch a fingerling mullet. They are visual hunters. Other birds such as the roseate spoonbill hunt by touch. The spoonbill sticks its sensitive bill in the sand, clamping down when it feels a small animal.

Most birds are now roosting in mangroves, or standing on one leg on shore, asleep with their heads tucked under their wings. Some hungry birds are still hunting. Some, with good night vision, continue visual hunting

With its sensitive beak, the roseate spoonbill can hunt by day or in the dark.

on all but the darkest nights. You can see them looking for food at the edges of the estuary. A few birds can shift from visual hunting to foraging by feel once the sun sets. The willet, a large sandpiper, does this. At night, it catches worms and crustaceans entirely by feel.

One kind of estuary bird is almost entirely nocturnal. The black crowned night heron sleeps in mangroves or other trees all day. Now, at night, you see a dark shape fly overhead and land on a strip of sand exposed by the low tide. Another perches on a low dock. These stocky herons probably evolved to avoid competition during the day with taller, more active herons and egrets. When they have eaten their fill, they return to their nests in the mangroves. The male picks the spot and brings sticks for the female to make the nest. They take care of three or four chicks.

Though many birds are asleep, there is new activity along the estuary coasts. Nocturnal animals such as raccoons and opossums come out of

their hiding places in trees or burrows and begin to forage along the shore of the estuary. Opossums will eat creatures stranded at low tide and the leftovers

The night heron specializes in nocturnal hunting.

Raccoons will forage in the mangroves along the edge of estuaries.

of other animals' meals. Raccoons will use their clever hands to search the shallow water near the mangrove roots for shrimp, crabs, and mollusks. They will dip the food they find in the estuary water. Sometimes, larger predators such as bobcats and coyotes will visit the edges of the estuary. This rich, productive ecosystem provides food for animals of the land and the sea.

Although many creatures are active through the night, others are sleeping or resting. Each has its own way to get the rest it needs. Sleep

SHARK SLEEP

Some sharks have to keep swimming all of their lives. They need to force water over their gills so they can breathe. These sharks can never truly sleep. Some other sharks, such as nurse sharks, have a way to keep water flowing over their gills even when they aren't moving. Nurse sharks often sleep on the bottom or under ledges.

is a time to heal the body after a day of surviving. During sleep, muscles build, repairs are made to damaged tissues, and the body makes many of the chemicals it needs. Sleep is even more important for the brain. While a creature sleeps, all of the experiences it has while awake are organized by the brain. This helps preserve memories and lets the animal learn from experience. (Some species are more capable of learning than

Manatees can rise to breathe without completely waking up.

others.) In mammals, it is believed that sleep is a time when the brain is actually cleaned. Brain cells shrink so that the area between them can be cleaned of waste products. It is unknown exactly what happens in the brains of fish when they rest or sleep, but it could be something similar.

Manatees sleep pretty much all the time. Many times throughout the day and night, manatees will swim down to the muddy or sandy bottom and sleep. Right now, you see several with their heads down, lying directly on the estuary floor. Usually, a manatee has to rise to the surface to breathe every few minutes. However, when they sleep, their heartbeat slows, and they can stay underwater for as long as twenty minutes. When they surface to breathe, they don't become fully awake. It is almost like a human sleepwalking. When manatees sleep in shallow water they are at risk of being hit by boats. Many manatees have scars from boat propellers. Many have been killed. They don't

TRANSPARENT EYELID

Fish don't have eyelids, but some sharks have a membrane they can see through that covers the eye for protection only when the shark is feeding. However, sharks don't close this special eyelid when they rest.

usually wake up when the loud boat comes near because their hearing doesn't pick up the sound that boat engines make.

Dolphins never get a full night's sleep. While manatees can stay almost asleep and still surface to breathe, a dolphin must be conscious to breathe. If a dolphin went fully to sleep, it would have to wake up every few minutes to breathe. Dolphins and whales have found a compromise: they only sleep with half of their brain at a time.

Scientists have monitored dolphin brains while they sleep and found that one half is always awake. This is enough to safely control breathing and prevent drowning. The other half of the brain can be deeply asleep. Very quietly, you paddle up to a small family of sleeping dolphins. You see that each has one eye closed and one eye open. The brain half on the opposite side from the closed eye is the one that is sleeping. (The left half of the brain controls the right half of the body, and vice versa.)

Fish also do something like sleep. They don't have eyelids, so they can't close their eyes. However, most fish enter a resting state that scientists think is their version of sleep. They will find a safe place and remain motionless. Some, like lizardfish or

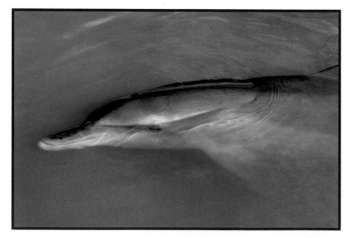

Dolphins only sleep with half of their brain resting at a time.

Some fish, such as wrasse and this parrotfish, make a mucus bubble to sleep in.

flounder, will burrow under the sand. You paddle over to the seagrass bed, where you see a small wrasse wrapped in a mucus bubble. The mucus comes from its mouth and goes around its body in a cocoon. This keeps other fish from detecting it and might help keep away parasites.

As you paddle home toward the bright lights of Tampa, you marvel that so much nature exists so close to an area of nearly three million residents. You hope people will take good care of their precious estuary.

WHERE ARE THE MAIN US ESTUARIES?

WEST COAST
- Padilla Bay, Washington
- South Slough, Oregon
- San Francisco Bay, California
- Elkhorn Slough, California
- Tijuana River, California

Lake Superior, Wisconsin

GREAT LAKES

Old Woman Creek, Ohio

Hudson River, New York

NORTHEAST
- Wells, Maine
- Great Bay, New Hampshire
- Waquoit Bay, Massachusetts
- Narragansett Bay, Rhode Island

MID ATLANTIC
- Jacques Cousteau, New Jersey
- Delaware
- Chesapeake Bay, Maryland
- Chesapeake Bay, Virginia

SOUTHEAST
- North Carolina
- North Inlet-Winyah Bay, South Carolina
- ACE Basin, South Carolina
- Sapelo Island, Georgia
- Guana Tolomato Matanzas, Florida
- Tampa Bay, Florida

Grand Bay, Mississippi

Weeks Bay, Alabama

Apalachicola, Florida

Mission-Aransas, Texas

Rookery Bay, Florida

GULF OF MEXICO

Kachemak Bay, Alaska

FAST FACTS ABOUT ESTUARIES

LOCATION: Estuaries are found all over the world. The Tampa Bay estuary is located on the west coast of Florida.

SIZE: Estuaries can be measured by surface area, or by miles of coastline. The two largest in North America are the Gulf of St. Lawrence in Canada, which has a surface area of 60,000 square miles (155,000 sq km), and

Chesapeake Bay, which has 11,684 miles (18,800 km) of coastline. Tampa Bay, the largest estuary in Florida, is 400 square miles (1,036 sq km).

TEMPERATURE: Estuaries can be found around the world wherever rivers feed into salt water. Thus, they can range from tropical to arctic climates. Water in the Amazon River estuary is usually higher than 70°F. Water in the Gulf of Ob estuary may be just above freezing.

RAINFALL: The amount of rainfall in estuaries varies, depending the location and the season. Estuaries in tropical regions get more rainfall than those in temperate or arctic regions. Heavy rainfall can lower the salinity of shallow estuaries.

PLANTS found in Florida estuaries include mangroves such as the red, black, and white mangrove, seagrasses such as turtle grass, shoal grass, and eel grass, seaweed/algae such as kelp, and drifting clumps of sargassum seaweed.

ANIMALS found in estuaries include mollusks: clams, oysters, scallops, lightning whelks, king's crowns, olive snails, and moon snails. Crustaceans include blue crabs, spider crabs, calico crabs, stone crabs, hermit crabs, and shrimp. Other invertebrates include octopus, squid, lugworms, starfish, and sea urchins. Fish include snook, redfish, mullet, sardines, herring, flounder, salmon, and eels. Sharks include bull sharks, hammerheads, bonnetheads, nurse sharks, and blacktips. Birds include seagulls, egrets, blue herons, night herons, cormorants, ducks, roseate spoonbills, ospreys, and eagles. Mammals include manatees, bottlenose dolphins, sea otters, seals, and sea lions. Beluga whales live in colder water.

GLOSSARY

aggressive Being always or often ready to attack.

blubber A thick layer of fat beneath the skin in many marine mammals.

brackish Water with a mixture of salt water and freshwater.

camouflage Using color, shape, or texture to blend into the environment.

decaying Rotting or decomposing through the action of bacteria or fungi.

ecosystem A community of interacting plants, animals, and other organisms, along with their environment.

estuary A body of water formed where a river flows into an ocean or sea.

euryhaline Capable of surviving in both freshwater and salt water.

fertilize To add male genetic material to female genetic material to create offspring.

forage To search over a large area for food.

frigid Very cold temperatures.

germinate When a seed puts out shoots and starts to grow.

gills Breathing organs of fish and some other animals, with which oxygen is taken from water.

glacier A slowly moving river of ice.

ice age A period of extreme cold when there are many glaciers.

invertebrate An animal that does not have a backbone.

larva The immature form of an animal, which usually looks different than the adult.

mangrove A bush or tree that grows in coastal areas and can tolerate salt water.

marine Having to do with an environment of salt water.

nutrients Something that provides food or other things needed for energy and growth.

osmosis The process by which water moves through membranes.

photosynthesis The process by which a plant uses energy from the sun to make food.

plankton Small or microscopic organisms that drift on ocean currents.

predator An animal that hunts other animals for food.

reef A ridge of coral, oysters, or rock found in shallow water.

salinity A measure of how much salt is in water.

sediment Small pieces of matter that settle on the bottom of a body of water.

sluggish Slow moving, or appearing tired.

spats Oyster larva that have attached to a surface.

sperm Male reproductive material that will join with an egg during fertilization.

tectonic plate The layers of Earth's crust that move.

tide The rising and falling movement of bodies of water in part due to the moon's gravitational pull.

transformation To have a change in appearance.

FIND OUT MORE

Books

Bell, David Owen. *Awesome Chesapeake: A Kid's Guide to the Bay.* Centreville, MD: Tidewater Publishers, 2008.

Rhodes, Mary Jo. *Life in a Kelp Forest.* New York: Scholastic, 2005.

Skerry, Brian. *Face to Face with Manatees.* Washington, DC: National Geographic, 2010.

Wojahn, Rebecca Hogue. *A Mangrove Forest Food Chain.* Minneapolis, MN: Lerner, 2009.

Websites

EPA—Estuaries

https://www.epa.gov/nep

The US Environmental Protection Agency posts a wealth of information about estuaries and also about the various programs dedicated to preserving them.

Kids Do Ecology—World Biomes: Estuaries

http://kids.nceas.ucsb.edu/biomes/estuaries.html

This site from the University of California–Santa Barbara has facts about the plants, animals—including humans—that live in and near estuaries. It also features links to even more information.

National Geographic Society: Estuary

http://nationalgeographic.org/encyclopedia/estuary

Find a wealth of information about estuaries around the world at this comprehensive site. It includes pictures of several kinds of estuaries and estuary life.

INDEX

Page numbers in **boldface** are illustrations.
Words in **boldface** are glossary terms.

ABOUT THE AUTHOR

Laura L. Sullivan is the author of more than forty fiction and nonfiction books for children, including the fantasies *Under the Green Hill* and *Guardian of the Green Hill*. She has written many books for Cavendish Square, including two titles in the A Day in the Ecosystem series.

PHOTO CREDITS

Cover, p. 1 Lone Wolf Photography/Shutterstock.com; p. 4 mariakraynova/Shutterstock.com; p. 6 Photodisc/DigitalVision/Thinkstock; p. 7 Franco Banfi/Barcroft Media/Getty Images; p. 8 USGS; p. 10 USEPA/Wikimedia Commons/File:Oyster bed close up (5984383105).jpg/CC PD; p. 12 Terry Moore/Stocktrek Images/Getty Images; p. 13 Rich Carey/Shutterstock.com; p. 14 Andrew J Martinez/Science Source/Getty Images; p. 15 jivz/iStock/Thinkstock; p. 16 WaterFrame/Alamy Stock Photo; p. 17 Liquid Productions, LLC/Shutterstock.com; p. 18 Dray van Beeck/Shutterstock.com; p. 20 (left) Michael Wood/Stocktrek Images/Getty Images; p. 20 (right) Brett Atkins/Shutterstock.com; p. 21 Andrew J. Martinez/Science Source; p. 22 Designua/Shutterstock.com; p. 23 Stacey Lynn Payne/Shutterstock.com; p. 24 apomares/E+/Getty Images; p. 25 Tui De Roy/Minden Pictures/Getty Images; p. 26 Doug Perrine/Photolibrary/Getty Images; p. 28 Steve Trewhella/Corbis Documentary/Getty Images; p. 30 (left) RainervonBrandis/iStock; p. 30 (right) Alastair Pollock Photography/Moment/Getty Images; p. 31 Bates Littlehales/National Geographic/Getty Images; p. 32 Jerry Trudell the Skys the Limit/Moment Open/Getty Images; p. 33 ROMEO GACAD/AFP/Getty Images; p. 34 jo Crebbin/Shutterstock.com; p. 36 Don Mammoser/Shutterstock.com; p. 37 Julia Knauer/Shutterstock.com; p. 38 Ethan Daniels/Shutterstock.com; p. 40 urosr/Shutterstock.com; p. 41 Luciano Candisani/Minden Pictures/Getty Images; p. 42 NERRS/NOAA/Wikimedia Commons/File:NERRS color map October 2010..pdf/CC PD.